AF615730

SERGIO ARAGONÉS

MAD® PANTOMIMES

A Time Warner Company

If you purchase this book without a cover you should be aware that this book may have been stolen property and reported as "unsold and destroyed" to the publisher. In such case neither the author nor the publisher has received any payment for this "stripped book."

WARNER BOOKS EDITION

Copyright © 1987 by Sergio Aragones and E.C. Publications, Inc.
All rights reserved.
No part of this book may be reproduced without permission.
For information address:
E.C. Publications, Inc.
485 Madison Avenue
New York, N.Y. 10022

Title "MAD" used with permission of its owner,
E.C. Publications, Inc.

This Warner Books Edition is published by
arrangement with E.C. Publications, Inc.

Warner Books, Inc.
1271 Avenue of the Americas
New York, N.Y. 10020

A Time Warner Company

Printed in the United States of America

First Printing: January, 1987

Reissued: May, 1992

10 9 8 7 6 5 4 3 2

ATTENTION SCHOOLS

WARNER books are available at quantity discounts with bulk purchase for educational use. For information, please write to: SPECIAL SALES DEPARTMENT, WARNER BOOKS, 1271 AVENUE OF THE AMERICAS, NEW YORK, N.Y. 10020.

TO DICK YOUNG
AND THE GOOD OL' DAYS!

1

(2)

3

1

2
WET
CEMENT

1
ATARI

2

3
ATARI

JK
ATARI

1
2
ANTARCTIC

3

4

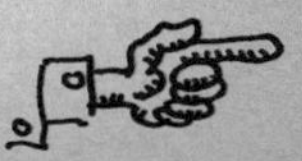

5

1

2

1

2

①
HELP!

(2)

3

4

2
VIVA
JESS
TOM
13
LA P

3

4
BANK

5
CASHIER

1

2

3

4

5

6

1

2
NUDIST
CAMP

1

2

@*!!

3

3
4

5
6

7

1

2

3

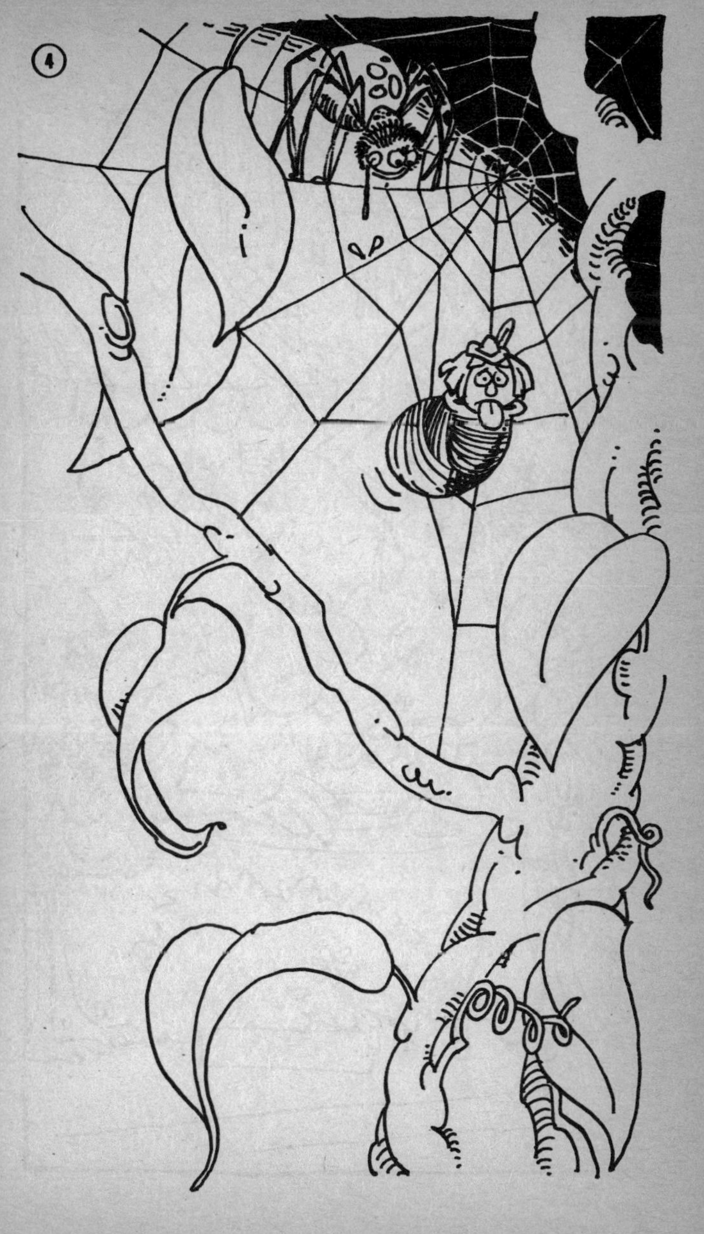
4

1
CAFE

2

3
TOURS
GET AWAY FROM THE CROWDS
DIVE!

4

5

6

①
水

(2)

1

2

3

T.V.
LOVE

1

3

5
CRACK!
SPLAT!

1
SSSSSS

②

3

1
2

3
4

5
6

7
8

1
ACME
RECORD
CO.

2
GREAT HIT
GOLD
GOLD

3
CONCERT

4
POSTER
LIFE
WHISKEY
PEOPLE
MUSIC
CASSETTE

5
POOF!

6
C. and C.
RECORDING
COMPANY

1
PET SHOP

2
LOVE DAD
MERRY CHRISTMAS MOM
TO JUNIOR FROM SIS
FOR MY LITLE BROTHER

1
BANG!
3

②

3

3

4
SNAP!

5

1
2
OUT

3
OUT
4

5

①

2
PLOP!

3

1

GRELL
SAFARIS

2

4

6

GRELL
SAFARIS

7

8

1

(2)

HUGE STUDIOS

3

3
MAKE UP
DEPT

4

1

2

3

ATOMIC
ATOMIC
WASTE

1
2
STOMP!
STOMP!
STOMP!

3
MINIATURE
$ CARS
10.00

②

3
NEXT GAS
10 MILES
GAS
4
GAS

5

6

1
PLASTIC
SURGERY
201

2

3

4
PLASTIC SURGERY
201

5
PLASTIC
SURGERY
201

1

2

(3)

69131

2010

(4)

2010

81

6

7

2018
02
81

8

2010
703

9

FINISH

2010

3789

10

FINISH

TV

2010

1

2

3

4

①

2

3

4

1
SERENDIPITY
TOY + HOBBY STORE
OJAI

2
F-104
STARFIRE
Revell
HMS BOUNTY
M60
A1
TAMIYA
BOEING
SST
B-25B
DNAGENTS
MODELS
EVANIER
TOYS
GROO
MINIATURES
BRIO

3
SIERRA
PYRO
ELSIE
STUKA
JUNKERS JU 87
1/32
Revell
MAD
PUTNAM
MODELS
Revell
HMS BOUNTY
H.M.S VICTORY
AIRFIX
Classic
Ships

1
TV

2
TV

3
PRUDENCE
THE TV GOURMET
CHEF
TV

4
DONUTS

1

2

3

4

5

6

7

8

9

2

③

①

2

3
SNAP!

4

1
ROCK
CONCERT
ARTIST
ENTRANCE

2
ROCK CONCERT
ARTIST ENTRANCE

1

3

(4)

1
COUNTY JUMPING FROG
JUBILEE
1000.00
FIRST PRIZ
FINISH

(2)

3

①

BIL STOUT
PALEONTOLOGICAL EXPEDITIONS

B.S.

②

3

4

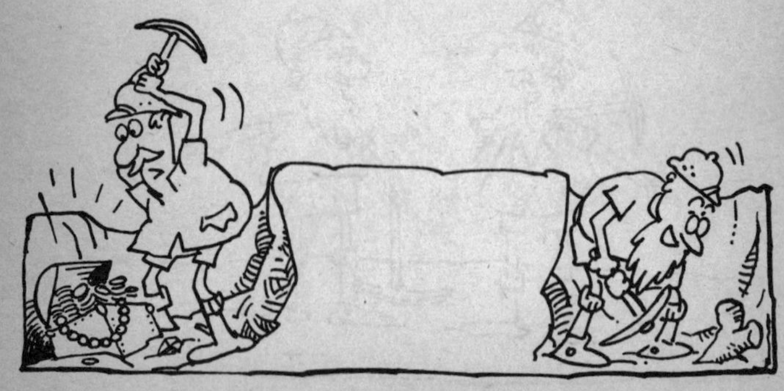

5
6

1

2

3

4

①

②

3

4

BZZZZ

2

3

1

2

3

4

5

①

②

3

4

1
2

5
6
SNAP!

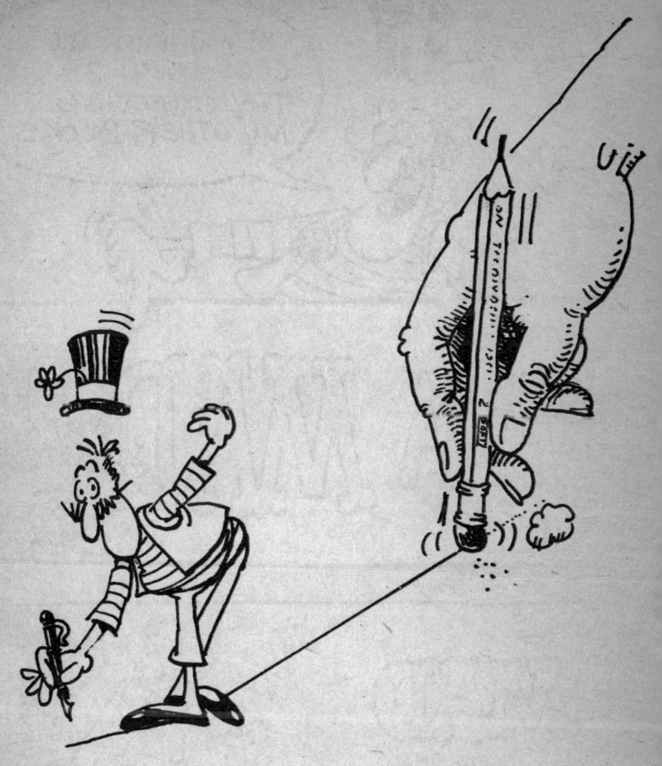

THE END

ARAGONÉS 86.

IF YOU THINK THOSE GAGS WERE BAD, TRY COLLECTING MY OTHER BOOKS!

VIVA MAD

IN MAD WE TRUST!

MAD MARGINALS!

MAD AS A HATTER!

MAD MENAGERIE

MORE
MARGINALS
GESUNDHEIT!
ARAGONÉS